*The adventures of Artie the Airplane
and his friends*™

Nothing Can Possibly
Go Wrong!

**Written and Illustrated
by
Captain Chuck Harman**

Early one morning, Artie the Airplane taxied out onto the ramp in front of his hangar. And, just like every other day, Jack the Jumbo and Frankie the Fighter joined Artie on the ramp to talk before going to work.

Suddenly, the still morning air at the Big Town airport was broken by a strange sound. "What's that, guys?" asked Frankie.

"I don't know what it is," replied Jack.

"Hmmm! Me, neither," said Artie.

"It sounds like a really fast plane—and you know how much I like really fast planes!" said Frankie.

As the noise got louder and louder, the three friends started looking all over the sky. "I still don't see anything," yelled Jack, "but it must be moving very fast!"

"He can't be THAT fast," said Frankie. "I'm not even THAT FAST!"

The boys were still looking high up in the sky when all of a sudden, a flashy plane roared over their heads!

"Whoa!" exclaimed Jack.

"Duck!" yelled Frankie.

Artie hit the ground and put his wings up over his head.

The plane then pulled up into a steep climb. All of the planes could hear him laughing over the roar of his motor. Then the little plane turned around to come in for a landing. Everyone taxied over to see who this new plane was.

"Hi, everyone!" he said. "My name is Bartholomew T. Barnstormer. I'm moving in here today and we're going to be neighbors!" Everyone gathered around Bart to welcome him to the Big Town airport.

Bart loved to show off. In fact, when he got ready to fly, he would taxi into position, rev up his engine to full power and shoot down the runway. Then, he would lift off and climb straight-up—and that was his normal takeoff!

When Bart returned to the airport after a long day at work, he would fly over the runway so low that all the other planes would hold their breath. They were afraid Bart might hit his propeller on the runway. Bart would go so fast that he would leave everything that wasn't stuck to the ground trailing behind him as he pulled up into a climb.

Bart would have a big smile on his face and a gleam in his eye. He hoped that everyone thought he was the greatest airplane that ever lived. Next, Bart would plan what scary stunt he would do for his landing. "Let's see," thought Bart. "Everyone will expect something big for the landing . . . I know, I'll come in upside-down. That will thrill them. They'll love it!"

Artie and some of the emergency vehicles would watch from the rescue ramp. They would get together to watch Bart's takeoffs and landings, hoping that they would never have to go rescue Bart because of one of his stunts.

Artie asked Pete the Patrol Car, "Do you think Bart would stop doing his stunts if we got him to understand how dangerous they are?"
Pete just said, "It can't hurt to try, Artie, but usually, something has to happen to planes like Bart before they are willing to listen."

Artie taxied over to Bart's hangar to talk. "Hi, Bart," said Artie. "I'm glad to see that you were able to make a safe landing today."
"I always do," said Bart.
"Have you ever thought about the stunts that you do?" asked Artie.
"They are not very safe and something could go wrong. You or someone else could get hurt."

Bart just laughed. "Artie, these stunts aren't unsafe, they just look that way. When I pull them off, everyone looks up to me and thinks I'm the greatest plane that ever lived."

"You know, Bart," said Artie, "the other planes like you for who you are, not for your crazy stunts."

Bart just laughed, "Sure they do, Artie, heh heh. I have to go now. I have to think about what I'm going to do tomorrow."

As Bart taxied into his hangar, Artie worried about him. "I don't think he believes me," thought Artie. "I hope he doesn't get hurt trying to impress everyone."

Very early the next morning, Bart roared off into the sky. He climbed up really high so that he could dive down and get going really fast. He was going to level off and streak along just above the ground. "This is going to look so good," thought Bart, as he started into the dive.

Bart pulled out of the dive just inches from the ground, rolled over on his back and streaked across the meadow. Everything was going just like Bart had planned. "This is great!" thought Bart. "Nothing can possibly go wrong!" Bart didn't know it then, but he was headed right for a fence!

"Sprong!" went the fence. When the dust settled, there was Bart, upside down and hopelessly tangled in the fence. "Uh-oh," thought Bart.

Later, as Bart lay tangled up in the fence, he could see big
thunderstorms building up over the mountains. "Oh no," thought Bart.
"I hope those thunderstorms don't come this way. That's the last thing
I need." Just then, Bart felt a drop or two of rain on his goggles. "This
is not a good sign," worried Bart. He had always been in his hangar
during big storms.

That evening, the planes waited for Bart's big afternoon arrival. Soon it was dark and Bart had not returned. Jack the Jumbo jumped up onto a small hill to look for Bart.

"I can't see him anywhere," said Jack. "We'd better go home and set our alarms. We'll need to get up early and start looking for Bart!"

As night fell, the storms moved closer to Bart. Next, the wind started to pick up. Soon a big storm was right over Bart. There was lots of wind and rain and lightning and thunder. All Bart could do was lie there, stuck in the fence, helpless, as the storm raged on during the night.

The next morning, Gramma Cubbie began organizing the search teams. "Artie, Jack and Frankie will fly north and south and look for Bart," she said. "Piper and Sigmund will fly east and west."
"Yes, ma'am!" they all answered. Everyone took off to look for Bart. They flew up one way for a few miles and then turned around and flew back.

Just after noon, Frankie told Artie and Jack that he would have to return to the airport to get more gas. "I'll be back as soon as I can," said Frankie as he turned toward the airport.

As Frankie flew toward the Big Town airport, he saw a flash of color
below him. He circled around and there was Bart, still tangled in the
fence. "Hi, Bart!" yelled Frankie. Are you okay?" Bart looked
relieved that Frankie had found him, but he was also very embarrassed
that one of his stunts had gone wrong.

"I'm okay, Frankie, but I could use a little help," said Bart. Frankie told Bart that everyone was out looking for him. "I'll radio the rescue center and tell them where you are. Help will be here in a few minutes, Bart," said Frankie. "I've got to get back to the field for some gas. I'll see you later."

The rest of the planes were waiting when Bart, Artie and Jack landed back at the airport. Everyone was so glad to see that Bart was okay. "Hmm," thought Bart. "Maybe Artie was right. Everyone is happy to see me and I didn't even do a big stunt. What's even more strange, I really messed up and they're still happy to see me. Maybe they do like me for just me and not my stunts."

Everyone crowded around Bart. "What happened, Bart?" asked Sigmund the Sky Crane.

"Bart, where were you all night? We were worried about you," said Artie's cousin, Piper.

"I spent the night tangled in a fence," Bart told everyone. "I thought that none of you would like me if I didn't do my crazy stunts. I'm sorry that I caused you all to worry about me so much."

That night Bart lay in his hangar thinking about what had happened to him. "I am one lucky plane," thought Bart. "Some of those stunts I used to do even scared me because I know how close I came to hurting myself. I'm glad I don't have to do them anymore."

The next morning, instead of showing off, Bart sat on the ramp eating Plane Toasties and having a wonderful time talking with his friends. "This is great," thought Bart. "Artie is right; it's who you are, not what you do that's important!"

Meet a few of

Alice the Air Ambulance

Albert T. Agplane

Becky the Big Tire Blimp

Bubba the Bush Plane

Carlos the Cargo Plane

Codi the Copter

Eduardo the Explorer

Frankie the Fighter

Gilda the Glider

Gramma Cubbie

Grampa Cubbie

Heidi the High Wing

Jack the Jumbo

Jessie the Jet Fuel Truck

Leslie the Low Wing

Artie's friends.

Pete the Patrol Car

Pierre the Plane

Piper

Robert the Rescue Plane

Lt. Sam Sweptwing

San Antonio Sal

Simon the Starfighter

Shirley the Skyvan

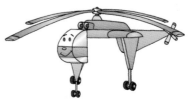

Sigmund the Skycrane

Superslim

Tina the Tailwheel

Waldo W. Wing

Wally the Widebody

Bartholomew T. Barnstormer

Captain Chuck

Artiefacts™

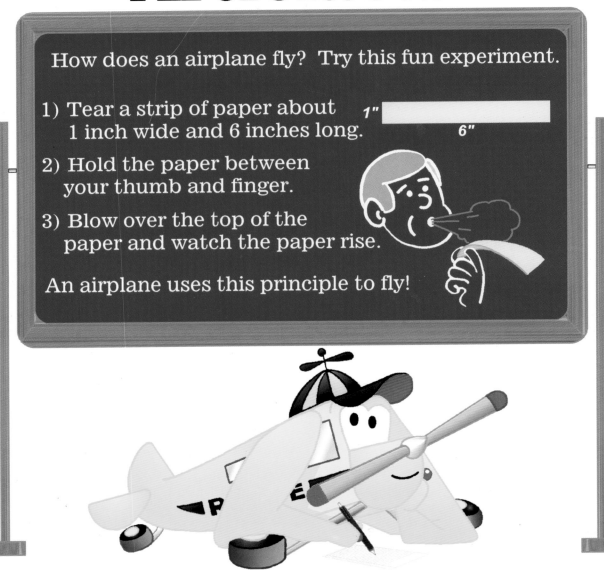

How does an airplane fly? Try this fun experiment.

1) Tear a strip of paper about
   1 inch wide and 6 inches long.

2) Hold the paper between
   your thumb and finger.

3) Blow over the top of the
   paper and watch the paper rise.

An airplane uses this principle to fly!

1"

6"